Jesus
Never Said
Everyone
Was
L♥vable!

D0067461

Jesus Never Said Everyone Was L♥vable!

Lessons in Discipleship

CLAY F. LEE

Abingdon Press

Nashville

Jesus Never Said Everyone Was Lovable!
Lessons in Discipleship

This book is printed on acid-free paper.

Library of Congress Cataloging-in-Publication Data

LEE, CLAY F. (Clay Foster), 1930–
  Jesus never said everyone was lovable!
  1. Love—Religious aspects—Christianity—Sermons.
  2. Methodist Church—Sermons. 3. Sermons, American.
  I. Title.
  BV4639.L385   1987   252′.076   86-25848
            ISBN 0-687-19980-8 (alk. paper)

"Minnie Remembers," from *Mind Song* by Donna Swanson, R. 1,
Williamsport IN 47993, is used by permission (pp. 45-46).
"Faith," from *The Best of Studdert-Kennedy* by G. A. Studdert-Kennedy,
Copyright renewed 1952 by Emily Studdert-Kennedy, is reprinted by
permission of Hodder and Stoughton Limited (pp. 101-2).
Lines from *Camelot* (p. 18) are Copyright © 1960 & 1961 by Alan Jay
Lerner & Frederick Loewe. Chappell & Co., Inc., owner of publication and
allied rights throughout the world. International Copyright Secured. All
rights reserved. Used by permission.

Scripture references noted NEB are from The New English Bible © the
Delegates of the Oxford University Press and the Syndics of the Cambridge
University Press 1961, 1970. Reprinted by permission.
Those noted KJV are from the King James Version.
All others are from the Revised Standard Version of the Bible,
copyrighted 1946, 1952, © 1971, 1973 by the Division of Christian
Education of the National Council of the Churches of Christ in the U.S.A.,
and are used by permission.

MANUFACTURED BY THE PARTHENON PRESS AT
NASHVILLE, TENNESSEE, UNITED STATES OF AMERICA

To my wife, Dot,
whose individuality and openness
have been a source of motivation through
thirty-five years of shared ministry

ACKNOWLEDGMENTS

The sermons in this book were not originally written and delivered as a series. Rather, they were brought together as a result of my being confronted by the challenge of submitting a series for possible use on "The Protestant Hour." Over the ten-month period during which I shared these twelve sermons with the congregation of Galloway Memorial United Methodist Church of Jackson, Mississippi, I was surprised by the way they seemed to fit together. It was as if, unconsciously, I had dealt with several of the varied themes involved in Christian discipleship. My instincts were confirmed many times over by the loyal people of the Galloway congregation.

Every United Methodist who has taken part in "The Protestant Hour" series knows that without the assistance, prodding, and guidance of Dr. David Abernathy, the task probably would never have been completed. What a joy it was to have him at my shoulder, encouraging when I needed it and reproving when I became slack. Preaching to one congregation over a period of years requires a great deal of discipline, but it cannot come close to the discipline required for a radio broadcast. I would have been totally lost without David Abernathy's great skill in communication.

I want to thank Bill Horlock and the other people at the Protestant Radio and Television Center in Atlanta, whose dedication to quality religious broadcasting has been a source of both inspiration and motivation.

I am also endebted to the staff members of Galloway Church, who have assisted in numerous ways. I want to pay particular tribute to Margie Greenough—for typing and retyping, for proofreading, and for the helpful attitude of patience—and to a longtime friend, Virginia Ables, who prepared the final manuscript.

I am particularly grateful to the Commission on Communications of the Southeastern Jurisdiction of The United Methodist Church, which chose me as the 1987 "Protestant Hour" preacher. A great deal of work was involved in the project, but it has been a labor of love.

Finally, I want to express appreciation to my wife for the part she has played in this endeavor, as well as in my entire ministry. She has kept me honest and helped me remember that no one individual can take credit for the Kingdom's results. Each of us has a part, and each part is necessary to complement and augment the other parts. I am continually brought back to reality by Paul's words: "I planted, Apollos watered, but God gave the growth" (I Cor. 3:6).

CONTENTS

INTRODUCTION

How would you answer the question, What is the purpose of Christianity? If your response reflected the traditional view, it would be something like this: "To proclaim the saving grace of God in Jesus Christ and to make disciples of all believers."

Such a response would not be overly debated by most Christians. Both mainstream Christians and those not considered mainstream could buy into that concept.

Why, then, are there so many differences within the body of Christianity? They result, at least in part, from the many different under-standings of what it means to be a disciple of Jesus Christ. Perhaps the situation in today's world is no different from situations in the past, but communication is much better today. We know what is going on not only in the church across the street but in the church on the other side of the world.

Our attempt to put into focus the full spectrum of discipleship is not intended to sell one particular denomination's viewpoint. Rather, it is an honest effort to deal with the total scope of discipleship so that we can better guard against narrow, provincial understandings.

It is my purpose to bridge two basic cornerstones of human reality: We are created with a need to be useful; and God needs and still seeks disciples who will cooperate in making his Kingdom a reality upon this earth.

Clay F. Lee
Jackson, Mississippi

Jesus
Never Said
Everyone
Was
L♥vable!

CHAPTER 1

Jesus Never Said Everyone Was Lovable!

(The Scope of Discipleship)

Mark 6:7-13

I read recently about a church in Southern California which had sponsored a refugee family from the Far East. In a matter of just a few months the refugees had cheated the church out of a rather large sum of money and a great many household goods.

Fortunately, that kind of situation is the exception rather than the rule. But we all know something about trying to be of help to others and having them take advantage of us. When that happens, we may feel as many of the members in that Southern California church did. They were angry. They felt they never again wanted to help anyone. But their pastor wisely counseled that service to others is not based on the expectation of gratitude, and people should not be surprised when the needy turn out to be sinners like everyone else.

This seems to be the very heart of Jesus' teaching as he sent his disciples on a mission of service. According to Jesus, service is not based on response. When he commissioned the disciples, he did not assign them to go only to the nice and appreciative. Indeed, as he described the mission they were to undertake, he did not intend that they preselect some target audience within a given community. Their ministry was to include everybody.

There are both clean and unclean human beings in need, solid citizens as well as those on the very fringe of society. Some are pleasant and nice; others are rude and hostile. Even the most gifted person must expect failure as well as success, pain as well as joy, rejection as well as acceptance.

This mission must have served as a rude awakening for those disciples. It occurred early in the ministry of Jesus, when I am sure they were caught up in idealistic dreams. They had even forgotten the rather abrupt rejection Jesus had just endured in his hometown of Nazareth. Now Jesus attempts to shock them into reality. Do they think they can compile a better record than his? In other words, they should be aware that they too will be rejected.

What about Jesus' instruction to "shake the dust" off their feet in reaction to rejection? Taking that expression only at its face value might lead us to believe that if the witness of the gospel were not immediately accepted, the disciples were to leave in disgust and find a more favorable audience. That was the attitude of the California church members: "Burn me once, shame on you! Burn me twice, shame on me!" However, that is not Jesus' message here.

Listen carefully: "At any place where they will not receive you or listen to you, shake the dust off your feet as you leave, as a warning to them" (6:11 NEB). When we dissect that statement carefully, we see that nothing is said about summarily slamming the door behind them. Nothing is said about an immediate departure. Indeed, there seems to be the strong suggestion that they have stayed for some time, in spite of the fact that they have not been listened to or appreciated.

Also, we need to put "shaking off the dust" in its proper historical perspective. It was more than a phrase used by Jesus. It was a customary Jewish gesture to show distaste. Jesus was instructing his disciples to use that gesture against the Jews themselves, and it was to be a gesture of warning.

The disciples' message was that God was now establishing his long-awaited reign over Israel. Every community, individual, and family must decide whether to join with Jesus in this new chapter of national history. Those who refused to join were in fact opting out of the New Age. According to Mark, Jesus instructed the disciples to use that familiar gesture as a warning to any who, by their own act, severed themselves from the covenant of grace God was offering.

Our inability to be patient in seeking both to understand and to serve may be one reason our progress in Christianity appears so slow. Sometimes the gospel seems to be offered as a take-it-or-leave it proposition. Such a demand for an immediate decision implies that God may never offer this bargain again.

There is no question as to the urgency of the gospel. But we must remember also that the Holy Spirit can work through patience much better than through impatience. The time may ultimately come when we, like the disciples of old, will shake the dust off our feet because the gospel has been rejected. But we must not do it in a condemning way. The warning must be offered in love, a love that grows out of concern for the seriousness of the gospel.

It is true that there is a temptation to serve only those who graciously respond. It is great to serve the grateful—their smiles and thankful eyes warm our hearts. But God calls us to serve ingrates also. Such persons share little or nothing with those who seek to serve them, but to exclude them would be to look for avenues of service through stained-glass eyes.

Perhaps that is one of the real barriers to Christian maturity. We keep thinking there is perfection in this world. Do you remember the description of Camelot in the musical of that name? Camelot was so perfect that

> The rain may never fall till after sundown.
> By eight the morning fog must disappear.
>
> . . . .
>
> The snow may never slush upon the hillside.
> By nine P.M. the moonlight must appear.

Few people would refuse to serve in such a

world, for if there were any needy folk at all, they would surely be perfectly nice people. But Camelot does not exist outside our imagination. We are called to live and love in an imperfect world, where the needy are not always nice, and all too many take rather than receive!

John F. Alexander, in a rather provocative article, "Do Old Drunks Sell Their Food Stamps?" pointed out that the vast majority of those who receive some form of public assistance are honest. They are trapped by circumstances over which they have no control. However, we cannot get away from the fact that there are those who cheat on public assistance and welfare programs. Alexander's conclusion was that

it is time to stop romanticizing the poor. . . . In my experience poor people are about like everyone else, maybe a little nicer, certainly less arrogant and more open to the gospel. Of course, they have their share of nastiness, just like the rest of us. . . .

Poor old drunks do sell their food stamps for cheap wine. . . . I don't say that because I'm mad at poor people. I say it because it's true, and if we're to work for justice we need accurate analysis. (*The Other Side* [June 1984]:8-9)

You may not respond positively to Mr. Alexander's evaluation. But those concerned with justice and compassion for the poor and needy would be better able to render service if they did stop romanticizing the whole issue. I believe the spirit of Jesus Christ is beautifully exemplified in Victor Hugo's classic *Les Miserables*. You remember the story—a French priest accepts a fugitive into his home, providing him shelter and food and friendship, only to have him run off one night with the valuable and sacred Communion vessels. The priest was neither surprised nor dismayed. He merely observed that the man was desperately in need of God's grace, as we all are, and left the matter in the hands of our Maker.

We who tend to think of ourselves as normal human beings would be faced with one of two temptations in such a circumstance. Either we would overly romanticize the conditions of the fugitive, or we would take the arrogant attitude that he was responsible for his condition and therefore we would not need to accept any responsibility for him. This leads, of course, to labeling people—good, nice, bad, nasty, irresponsible, and so on. By such an effort we cut one another off from the clear facts of our humanity, which are more complex than simple labeling can ever capture. It is this practice that opens the trap into which otherwise well-intentioned religious people tend to fall—serving only those who seem to be deserving or appreciative.

Is this some hypothetical question? Are we belaboring the wrong issue? I remember an ethics course in which a hypothetical question was raised: Suppose you are in an overloaded lifeboat in the middle of the ocean. In order for the boat to stay afloat, one person of the thirteen aboard must leave. There are no life preservers. Which of these thirteen people would you choose to try to make it alone: the captain of the ship, a ten-year-old girl whose parents went down with the ship, a pregnant woman, a sailor with a reputation for drunkenness, a member of the Mafia, the ship's cook, an elderly passenger with a terminal illness, a wealthy playboy, a clergyman, a critically wounded passenger, an idiot, or a nurse?

How would you even begin to make such a decision? Given those circumstances, I have a feeling each of those people could give a strong argument as to why he or she should not be the one chosen. Should they draw straws and simply leave so serious a matter to chance? This is exactly the dilemma the church faces when it tries to decide who it will save in its evangelistic mission. Many churches feel they have such limited funds and energies, they cannot reach everyone. Inevitably those who are thought of as losers are avoided as if they had the plague.

Recall Jesus' instructions to his disciples. They were not to weigh themselves down with a lot of paraphernalia. Their approach to the task of making the kingdom of God known was to be that of utter simplicity, complete trust, and the generosity that always gives and never demands. It is only after all these things were fulfilled that the disciples had any choice. If they were not well received, they could leave that place and move on. The decision had nothing to do with the type of audience. In fact, the warning here was that no choice should be made. The gospel of Jesus Christ is for both the lovable and the unlovable, the appreciative and the unappreciative, the nice and the nasty.

A strong lesson for us in the church today is found in Jesus' instructions to his disciples as he sent them out on that initial venture. We do need to struggle with that temptation of choosing whom to serve. More particularly, we need to wrestle with the temptation of hoarding God's goodness, making it our own personal possession.

Let me tell you about a tribe in Africa known as the Masai, a race of strong, tall people. This particular tribe has always believed in one god, Engai. They believe Engai is passionately involved in his people's lives; that he loves the rich more than the poor, the healthy more than the sick, the virtuous more than the wicked. Engai favors the Masai over every other tribe, providing them with rain and sleek cattle and protecting them against their enemies.

You could almost call that attitude primitive if it were not for the fact that such a view of God is held by many people in our society today. Our lesson is to capture Jesus' understanding of God. We are to respond with simplicity and trust and generosity, just as Jesus instructed his disciples. Then we will be on the road to the Kingdom.

Selectees . . . or Selectors?

(The Selection of Discipleship)

Ephesians 1:1-10

In past times of national crisis, every able-bodied man who did not volunteer was drafted into the armed services. This draft was administered by the Office of Selective Service. Many young men said they were glad to serve their country, but they did not understand the terminology: They did not do the selecting. They were the selectees . . . not the selectors!

My high school geometry teacher had quite a reputation for strict teaching methods. There is no question that she struck fear into the hearts of many students, myself included. She would say, "I want three volunteers to go to the board and work this problem! [And before anyone could raise a hand, she would indiscriminately point.] You . . . you . . . and you." Somehow, just as the Office of Selective Service did not allow one to select, that teacher's method just did not fit into our understanding of volunteering.

This same concept presents a dilemma for some people in their spiritual lives. Do we choose how we shall serve our Lord's kingdom, or are we chosen for a specific service? Actually, there should be no dilemma. There is a sense in which we both choose and are chosen. An awareness of the way this is lived out in our daily lives is essential to spiritual health and maturity.

To begin with, we are chosen! That God has taken the initiative in reaching out to us is a distinguishing characteristic of the Christian faith. Most world religions believe in some concept of God—that there is some great power and strength which exceeds our human lives. However, in so many of the world religions, the concept of divinity is removed from the day-to-day life of ordinary human beings. God is elusive, and the purpose of life is to search out the Divine.

But not so in the Christian faith. We affirm that God has made the first step—not away from us, but toward us. As Jesus said to his disciples, "You did not choose me, I chose you." Or as the apostle Peter describes the believers in Jesus Christ: "You are a chosen race, a royal priesthood, a holy nation, God's own people, that you may declare the wonderful deeds of him who called you out of darkness into his marvelous light. Once you were no people but now you are God's people; once you had not received mercy but now you have received mercy" (I Peter 2:9-10).

And this is the basic theme expressed so eloquently in Paul's letter to the Ephesian Christians. He says we should bless God, "who has blessed us in Christ . . . even as he chose us in him before the foundation of the world, that we should be holy and blameless before him" (1:3b, 4). Yes, we are the selectees, not the selectors!

What a basis for life this is! "Before the foundation of the world," we were in the heart and mind of God. That is our stepping-off spot, our starting place. There is no reason for us to develop some earthshaking doctrine about this. No, we can let it simply rest there while we ponder the magnificent mystery in which we are involved. Indeed, we should breathe very slowly while pondering this mystery. Let it sink in: *I am from the foundation of the world, from the mind and heart of God. God is my home, I am at home with God—all because God has acted to make it that way!*

If we could digest this mystery, it undoubtedly would give us a more comprehensive view of what it means to be a human being in the here and now. It would soothe that nagging feeling that we are simply earthbound relics confined to time and space. But because we are chosen, we know we are not prisoners of time and space. We are much more—we are the substance of God and creation! And we are involved also in the redemptive process that will open our eyes to this reality, so we can be brought into a deeper consciousness of God, and of ourselves. That important question, Who am I? is answered competently and clearly in this realization. We are the chosen ones, chosen before the world was founded. We were, we are, and we shall be always in the mind of God, with all that implies.

If God chose us, he must have had a reason. Are we such perfect objects of creation that our

Maker stands in awe of us, as we would gasp in the presence of a perfect jewel? Of course not! God chose us in spite of our imperfection, as a part of his eternal plan for the fullness of time. He chose us "to unite all things in him, things in heaven and things on earth" (1:10*b*).

God's choice is always for a productive purpose. We have a basic, practical value. We are co-laborers with God, to use Paul's terminology. From the beginning of time God has wanted us to work with him toward the perfection of this world. And although God is pleased when we joyously choose to cooperate with him in his purpose, he chose us first.

The unthinking person might assume that since God took the initiative—that is, was the Selector while we are the selectees—our human will has no value in this matter. God took the initiative, but it was just that: a beginning. He's saying to us, "I believe in you. I need you to help me bring my world to completion. I want you to accept your *chosenness*. I want you to respond joyously and gladly."

Most of us do not react negatively to being chosen. Indeed, if that were all there is to this whole matter of discipleship, we could be much more enthusiastic about it. But the choice is one of responsibility, not privilege. The deeper we go into our discipleship the more we are called to risk. A journey away from the familiar and secure can be very frightening.

Of this we must be sure—if we accept our

chosenness we must have a clear understanding of what it involves. When we say yes to this noble affirmation, we are saying there is logic and meaning and value in God's aim for this world. We are affirming that history is the working out of the will of God, that God has given up neither on his creatures nor on his creation, that there is something that makes sense even in a world of senseless happenings.

The tragedy is that many persons simply refuse to accept the idea that God is working out his pupose by choosing and using our frail human lives. They see nothing but darkness and gloom. In his preface to *A History of Europe*, H.A.L. Fisher writes: "One intellectual excitement, however, has been denied me. Men wiser and more learned than I have discovered in history a plot, a rhythm, a predetermined pattern. These harmonies are concealed from me. I can see only one emergency following upon another as wave follows upon wave" (Houghton Mifflin Co., 1939).

There is a desolate tone to such a confession. One is reminded of a similar statement of despair in the *Memoirs* of the French author André Maurois, written when he learned of the assassination of John F. Kennedy:

We anxiously question a world we have pictured in our minds; we imagine dialogues between heads of state; we are fearful, we worry, we make plans, we wait for an answer; and he who could perhaps have given the answer dies because an inexplicable plot placed in the hands of an obscure nobody a rifle with telescopic sights and the nobody at once carried his secret into the shadows. "The

27

woes we fear do not come," said my friend Jean Rostand.
"Worse ones do." ([Harper & Row, 1970], p. 416)

We are living in an age when human beings
are tempted to lose faith in any purpose for this
world. There is no sense in the midst of never
ending senseless happenings! But the Christian
has faith that God's purpose is being worked out.
It was the conviction of the apostle Paul that this
purpose would someday be brought to fulfillment, that all things and all people would be one
family. The world was not even conscious of that
mysterious purpose until the advent of Jesus
Christ; now it is the great task of the church to
accept God's choosing and work toward the
fulfillment of God's desire for unity.

This is a revelation that can change our whole
outlook. Here is a majestic understanding of both
God and self that lifts us to the level of meaningful
and purposeful service.

A sermon by Thomas Hilton, the senior
minister of First Presbyterian Church in Pompano
Beach, Florida, is titled "Nickled and Dimed to
Death." You might think it would be a tirade on
chintzy giving patterns, but it actually is about
that eternal mystery in which God chooses us to
be his co-laborers. Until we are caught up in the
majesty of that mystery, we are tempted to
"nickle and dime" God to death in the service of
his kingdom. Like the advertising for a hair
preparation several years ago, we are convinced
that a little dab will do it. God's choice of us
for service in his kingdom is not a hit-and-run

proposition. It is a day-in-day-out matter of faithfulness. Paul sought to catch the attention and understanding of the Ephesians. When we know who it is that has chosen us, and the majesty of that purpose, which spans much more than just one brief lifetime, then we are prepared to say, "Here am I, Lord. . . . Send me. . . . Use me."

That sounds good, doesn't it? But, "Send me where, Lord? What do you want me to do?"

And here is the answer: Respond where you are. Do for others in the same manner and spirit you would do for God.

In Westminster Abbey, London, there is a memorial plaque to John and Charles Wesley, on which are recorded three quotations that symbolize what God's choice meant to those two brothers:

"The best of all, God is with us." These last reported words of John Wesley remain as his final affirmation of faith.

"The world is my parish." Here we are reminded that John and Charles Wesley accepted God's choice and understood that there was an eternal purpose "to unite all things in him, things in heaven and things on earth."

"God buries his workmen, but carries on the work." The responsibility for doing our part in the achievement of God's purpose is placed squarely upon us, the inheritors of the faith. We are the selectees. God is the Selector!

CHAPTER 3

A Style Without a Story

(The Source of Discipleship)

II Samuel 18:24-33

Some of us are old enough to remember the difficult days of the Second World War. There was a prevailing fear in homes from which fathers, sons, brothers, or husbands had left to fight in that war. The fear was that someone would open a telegram and see the words, "We regret to inform you . . . ."—words that could freeze the emotions of human beings.

Such telegrams were known as death notifications. Of course, delivery of death notifications is not confined to wartime. Police, sheriffs, coroners, military agencies, and clergy say it is one of the most intimidating services they are called upon to perform.

I mention this loathsome reality to introduce our Scripture lesson, for the story concerns the delivery of a death notice.

David, king of Israel, now well advanced in years, has seen Israel come a long way. When he began his reign, there was one tribe to deal with, and he was plagued by only the petty disturbances and disagreements that arose among that small group of people. However, those days are far gone. Now David administers a complex government, a large army, and complicated relationships with other nations, as well as an extended household of his own.

To make matters worse, his oldest son, Absalom, has instituted a plot against him. When David learns Absalom has gathered a rebel army at Hebron, he flees the city of Jerusalem. David makes a pathetic picture, barefoot and weeping, as he travels over the Mount of Olives toward the Jordan River. He is heartbroken by his son's action and grieved to learn that some of his most trusted friends have deserted him.

However, David is still a warrior at heart, and it takes only a short time to regroup his own army and map his strategy. He wants to lead the army himself, but the three generals whom he trusts persuade him to remain behind while they battle the forces of Absalom. David agrees and gives his generals only one specific order: "Deal gently for my sake with the young man Absalom."

The battle takes place in a thickly wooded area east of the Jordan River. Low-branched trees and exposed roots make it so difficult to get about that many soldiers are injured or trampled. "The forest devoured more people that day than the sword."

Absalom, the son of David, was a victim of the forest. When his long hair caught in the low-hanging branches, his mount kept moving, jerking him from the saddle. "He was left hanging between heaven and earth." David's generals threw his body in a pit and covered it with a great heap of stones. The battle was over and Absalom's rebel army was defeated.

It was now necessary to send a runner back to David to tell him that though his kingdom had been preserved, his son had been killed. Two runners were available to carry the report—Ahimaaz and a Cushite. Now, Ahimaaz could run faster than the Cushite, so he pushed forward when it was time for the general to make the assignment.

"Let me run, and carry tidings to the king," he cried.

But Joab, the general in charge, felt that someone other than Ahimaaz should deliver this delicate news—someone who could remember why he was running while he was running.

He said to Ahimaaz, "You may carry tidings another day, but today you shall carry no tidings, because the king's son is dead." ·

So Joab turned to the Cushite and told him to leave at once and tell King David "what you have seen."

You might think that was the end of the story, but it was not. Ahimaaz was not that easily put off. He pleaded some more, and although Joab was too worried to be sympathetic, he finally capitulated and Ahimaaz was off, running like a young deer. He passed the Cushite and arrived in the presence of David before the Cushite was even in sight.

King David was eager for news, but of course Ahimaaz did not know how to tell the king his son had been killed, so he improvised—"All is well!" But that was not what David wanted to know.

"Is it well with the young man Absalom?" he asked, and when Ahimaaz could not answer, David waved him aside.

By this time the slow, plodding Cushite had arrived. He gave a simple, coherent account of what had happened in the battle and how the victory had been won.

And when David asked the awful question, "Is it well with the young man Absalom?" the Cushite knew how best to break the tragic news: "May the enemies of my lord the king, and all who rise up against you for evil, be like that young man" (vs. 32*b*). It was news that was not easy to deliver, but the Cushite did it as delicately as possible.

And David responded with the shattering grief that only a parent can feel: "O, my son Absalom, my son, my son Absalom! Would I had died instead of you."

However, it is not the father in this ancient story who is the focal point of our attention, but the minor character Ahimaaz: He wanted to relate news he really did not know. His situation, both interesting and tragic, was similar to that of the young novelist who took his first manuscript to H. G. Wells, the critic. When the manuscript was returned several weeks later the young writer quickly opened it to learn the famous critic's opinion. On the last page he finally found one notation: "Style without story." This was true also of Ahimaaz. He had a style, but no story.

Perhaps Christian disciples have that chronic problem. It is possible for us to have a style without a story, a form without a faith, a willingness without a witness.

One day Jesus was confronted by a young man, and as the conversation ensued we are told that Jesus was drawn to him. I have always thought this meant that Jesus saw in this young man great emotional, mental, and moral potential. When the young man asked Jesus the one question that has the possibility of opening the door to eternal salvation, Jesus began by telling him to keep the commandments.

"All these I have observed from my youth," the young man replied.

Then Jesus said, "One thing you lack: go, sell everything you have . . . and come, follow me" (Mark 10:21b NEB).

You know the end of the story. What seemed to be leading to a gigantic climax suddenly fizzles. The young man walks away from the challenge. He had a style without a story. He had a form with no faith to fill it. Jesus' call to discipleship was too costly for him.

At another time, Jesus kept a private rendezvous with one of the Jewish leaders. Nicodemus had evidently been turned on by what he had heard from Jesus. He was inquisitive and kept asking questions that dealt with our human destiny. Jesus replied by saying that one must be born again (John 3:3). The Scripture does not tell us whether Nicodemus did in fact make a commitment, but we are led to believe he may later have done so, since he brought "myrrh and aloes" for Jesus' burial (John 19:39). Nicodemus may have added a story to his style.

Other moments recorded in the Gospels tell that Jesus was thrilled by the inner faith he discovered in people. Matthew, for example, tells of an unnamed Canaanite woman who begged Jesus to intercede in her daughter's behalf. His disciples uged him to send the woman away, and even Jesus reminded her that his most immediate mission was to the people of Israel.

Speaking figuratively, Jesus said, "It is not right to take the children's bread and throw it to the dogs."

The woman replied, "True, sir, and yet the dogs eat the scraps that fall from their masters' table."

And Jesus perceived her inner faith: "Woman, what faith you have! Be it as you wish!" (Matt. 15:28 NEB).

Faith was always the determining factor— not the outward show displayed. Not how zealous persons might seem, but to what extent they were willing to lay their lives on the line for what they believed. In the Old Testament story, the zealous man who begged to be given the task was unable to complete it; the individual drafted for the task accomplished it in unquestioning obedience. No one questions which was more valuable.

To acquire faith, we must be willing to experiment with what we have been told is the truth about God in Jesus Christ and make it our own. If Jesus honors our simple, honest trust, then we must dare to experiment with simple, honest trust in our lives. The gospel proclaims that God loves us so much that no matter how far we have strayed, how long we have stayed, or how jaded our souls, he is like an anxious father, waiting to welcome his child home again. It is one thing to talk about forgiveness; it is another to put it to the test. Until then, it is a style without a story.

But once we have acquired this faith, we must give it away. Ahimaaz was right in wanting to take the news of the battle to King David. Yet in the last analysis, the only real messenger is one who has a message to deliver and does so with all the sincerity and sensitivity the human spirit can capture. This is every person's opportunity and responsibility. It does not need to be done in the same place or in the same way by all individuals. Indeed, it is this diversity, and the uniqueness of each person's witness, that give the gospel its great appeal.

The consequences of a religion that is only form and style, without faith and story, are self-evident. That kind of religion highlights the gloss and glitter, looks for zeal and sensation, but has no inner framework of strength to hold it together in the time of testing.

What good does it do to run if we do not know why we are running? Of what value is a faith that has no inner strength? A style without a story has no lasting power. Unlike the Cushite who brought sad news to David, you and I have Good News to make known. It is the good news of God's love which forgives, redeems, remakes. When we have experienced that good news ourselves, then we have a story to tell—a story to which we can contribute our own God-given style. And that is what changes the world!

CHAPTER 4

Alone . . . in a Sea of People

(The Sensitivity of Discipleship)

Matthew 22:34-40

The person who said "We must learn to love one another or die" was certainly echoing the message of Jesus. When confronted by the Pharisees with the question, "Which is the greatest commandment?" (in other words, "What is the rule by which we ultimately live and die?"), Jesus answered that we must love God with every resource of our being and love our neighbor as ourself.

Consider that scene for a moment. Who were the Pharisees? They were arch legalists, men of intellect. Yet, even from their perspective, Jesus had answered correctly. Love is the greatest commandment. The Pharisees knew the Old Testament. It was written down that way, and these men, as scriptural lawyers, couldn't get around it. That was not the point of contention. Rather, it was a question of whether they actually lived that love.

On other occasions Jesus dealt with the Pharisees concerning the way they did or did not act on the principle of love. He made the point that all the law in the world, if put into practice in a rigid and mechanical way, would not bring them one step closer to God without some lubricant of mercy, some modicum of feeling and forgiveness.

It is probable that we have not always been as honest in our thoughts about the Pharisees as we should. Reports from that era suggest that of all the sects, the Pharisees seemed the most honest, sincere, even the friendliest and most optimistic. It is possible that Jesus debated them because he believed they really had some chance of being won over. They were not hopeless cases.

So consider the possibility that the Pharisees who came to Jesus that day were honest and pious, but who, like many of us, had their heads screwed on backward about a number of issues. When our basic perception is warped, then for all our honesty and good intentions, we are bound to go off in warped directions.

What was the problem with these honest Pharisees? Well, it is right there in the Great Commandment. These arch upholders of the Law knew they were supposed to love God and their neighbor. Well and good!

But the next question is the difficult one: How do you do it? Do you just get out of bed one morning and suddenly feel a gush of affection for the Lord on High? Do you suddenly look across the fence at your neighbor and forget every loud party he has ever thrown, and all the beer bottles that ended up on your side of the fence, and his dog that keeps digging in your flower bed? Do you, for the first time, see him as a child of God, a thing of infinite spiritual beauty? Well, do you? Or is your response, "For heaven's sake, let's be realistic!"?

Jesus was being realistic. The old adage that familiarity breeds contempt could well be true in this situation. We are so familiar with this passage, we never dig beneath the surface to grasp what Jesus is revealing. The question was, "How do we love God?" And Jesus answered, "Love your neighbor." Although this seems simple enough, we really do need to probe the deeper implication.

What if God actually came to us in human form? Would it be possible to love God as we love a human? In fact, that is the only way it *is* possible for us to love God, for God on High is a peerless abstraction, an unfathomable thing our human minds cannot visualize. Here is the real principle: The only way we can start loving God is by loving human beings.

So, by enunciating that age-old commandment, Jesus was infusing it with new meaning. He was revealing himself as the ultimate human model through whom mortals can know and love God: "No one comes to the Father, but by me" (John 14:6b). To those who knew and loved Jesus, that was exactly what he was—not just their Master, not just a beloved Companion, but a means by which they could know and love God.

Jesus was saying to the Pharisees, very

subtly, that God could become accessible to them, in a way they could identify and be attracted to, only through other human beings.

The dilemma of the Pharisees is ours also. We feel we should be able to grasp the reality of God on a purely intellectual basis. Perhaps that is possible for some; however, that knowledge will not enable us to love God. We can appreciate, respect, even offer obedience to God, but that does not necessarily mean we will love God.

Our American mind-set gets in the way at this point. In our sense of self-sufficiency we feel we should be able to march right up to God and say, "Look, I just want to become one with whatever it is you are, but I don't really want to get involved. So what's the trick? How do I get it without getting personally tied up in this?" That is, of course, the old American notion that we ought to be able to buy anything we want, with no strings attached.

But Jesus says it cannot happen without personalization, the creation of meaningful relationship. If we want faith in God to be pristine and structured and emotionally unengaging, then we are simply out of luck. Faith depends upon the creation, maintenance, and nurturing of a personal relationship with Jesus Christ.

I read recently that, according to the manufacturers, of the tremendous number of computers bought for home use, most simply are not being used. People paid good money for them but don't take the trouble to learn how to use them.

Consumer reports say something similar happened when rock music was introduced some years ago. Teenagers rushed out and bought musical instruments, only to discover that they still had to learn how to play them. To make a computer or a guitar or any other thing work requires a commitment, an investment of time and energy.

The same is true with God and with other people. They are strangers to us until we make a commitment and work at establishing a lasting relationship. God and people can be put on a shelf alongside a guitar we never learned to play. Isn't it a haunting thought that our ultimate choice when dealing with God and our neighbors is either to lose them to loneliness or to crown them with love?

It is not that the multitude of people who have lost their neighbors to loneliness do not come into contact with other human beings. No, they engage in commerce and recreation, and the pursuit of happiness just as others do. It is simply that love (like God) is an abstraction. They are alone in a sea of people. Or to put it in more positive terms, they are alone in a sea filled with potential relationships.

Neighbor love, as described by Jesus, is not based on moral sentimentalism; it is based on common humanity and the realization that we all, at some time, are estranged to some degree. Neighbor love is based on our common vulnerability to suffering, weakness, death, and

43

participation in sin. Because this is our common state of being, there is no reason anyone should ever feel alone.

On a 1984 television news program, I saw Michael Jackson arriving at the Denver airport in his private jet. When he got off the plane he was so hidden by the six burly men who surrounded him, he could hardly be seen.

I learned more about the young singer when I read an article in *The New Republic* (April 16, 1984). The Jacksons' father began training them when Michael was five years old. They worked two to three hours a day. During his teen years, when most children are facing the requirement to act more mature and rational, Michael Jackson was "getting positive feedback for remaining child-like." He developed a weird look, a falsetto voice, and an eccentric style of dress. Asked if he minded appearing schizophrenic, he answered, "I don't mind. I feel I'm Peter Pan as well as Methuselah" ("Prisoner of Commerce," p. 4).

That kind of situation doesn't seem to bother a lot of people. After all, they would say, look at the by-products—great wealth, a popularity that rivals that of Elvis Presley. In our childhood dreams, we fancy ourselves dealing with such problems; but in the world of reality, most of us would not trade our basic sense of relationship, the blessing of not feeling lonely, for all the money in the world.

Loneliness is a disease worse than cancer.

Cancer may destroy one's body, but loneliness can destroy one's spirit. You may be familiar with Donna Swanson's poem "Minnie Remembers." It focuses on the desperate loneliness felt by many people today, a loneliness that creates an unde-served burden for older adults. Picture an elderly woman sitting alone in a room, perhaps a room in a nursing home. She speaks softly to herself:

God,
My hands are old.
I've never said that out loud before
but they are.
I was so proud of them once.
They were soft
like the velvet smoothness of a
firm, ripe
peach.
Now the softness is like worn-out sheets
or withered leaves.
When did these slender, graceful hands
become gnarled, shrunken claws?
When, God?
They lie here in my lap,
naked reminders of this worn-out
body that has served me too well!

How long has it been since someone touched me?
Twenty years?
Twenty years I've been a widow.
Respected.
Smiled at.
But never touched.
Never held so close that loneliness
was blotted out.

. . . .

I remember the first boy who ever kissed me.

We were both so new at that!
The taste of young lips and popcorn,
the feeling inside of mysteries to come.

I remember Hank and the babies.
How else can I remember them but together?
Out of the fumbling, awkward attempts of new
lovers came the babies.
And as they grew, so did our love.
And, God, Hank didn't seem to mind
if my body thickened and faded a little.
He still loved it. And touched it.
And we didn't mind if we were no longer beautiful.
And the children hugged me a lot.
Oh God, I'm lonely!

God, why didn't we raise the kids to be silly
and affectionate as well as
dignified and proper?
You see, they do their duty.
They drive up in their fine cars;
they come to my room to pay their respects.
They chatter brightly, and reminisce.
But they don't touch me.
They call me "Mom" or "Mother"
or "Grandma."

Never Minnie.
My mother called me Minnie.
So did my friends.
Hank called me Minnie, too.
But they're gone.
And so is Minnie.
Only Grandma is here.
And God! She's lonely!

Do you understand the real depth of that
question—What is the ultimate rule and principle

by which we live and die? Jesus might have said, "Love God with every resource of your being and your neighbor as yourself." And he might well have added, "Then you will live! Then you will no longer be alone in a sea of people!"

CHAPTER 5

Let's Go Fishing!

(The Style of Discipleship)

Matthew 4:18-23

For many years my father was an avid fisherman. He was not an angler—he was a fisherman. He never owned a rod and reel, or a fly rod, or any other type of fancy equipment. He was a cane-pole fisherman. In fact, I have seen him manage as many as four poles at one time while sitting in a boat. Some of my fondest memories are of our fishing trips to the Pascagoula River.

I have always thought of those fishing expeditions as simply times of enjoyment, brief vacations from whatever responsibilities we would otherwise have had. Only in recent years have I come across a number of references to styles of fishing used as a means of evaluating human character.

Anthropologists tell us the pastime of fishing is over 500,000 years old. Primitive people, of course, fished to obtain food, but today most people fish for the fun of it. And that is probably a pretty good thing, given the luck most of us have with hook and line.

Aside from food and fun, fishing—over the years—has provided considerable insight into human character. I am referring not to the proverbial fabrications fishermen are famous for, but revelations of the inner person that pop out on a fishing trip.

Herbert Hoover, the most avid angler of all our presidents, said the surest way to get to know people was to take them fishing. If a person has any rascally traits, they will surely surface on a fishing trip.

One father commented that if a young man had serious designs on one of his four daughters, he didn't hire a genealogist to check the boy's family tree. Instead, he took him fishing—not to see how good a fisherman he might be, but what kind of man he was.

This may have been the thought pattern Jesus was following when he chose his first disciples, for he picked them from among fishermen. Peter and Andrew were fishing one day when Jesus walked by the Sea of Galilee. We can imagine Jesus watching them, perhaps noting something about their character as they fished, for he invited them to become his followers. Farther down the shore, Jesus watched another set of brothers fishing and issued the same invitation. So James and John, too, gave up their fishing to become "fishers of men." Evidently, in these four fishermen Jesus observed something basically solid that could be molded into something good, and he netted them for the kingdom of God.

In *The Gospel of Matthew* (Daily Study Bible Series [Westminster Press, 1977], pp. 78-79), William Barclay enumerates those qualities he thinks Jesus saw in Peter, Andrew, James, and John.

Good fishers must have the patience to wait until a fish takes the bait. I remember my father saying, "Don't jerk the pole the moment the cork begins to bob in the water. Wait until the cork goes all the way under, then pull on the line." I am afraid my impatience was as evident then as it is now. I have often said I can preach with power on patience, but my own leaves a lot to be desired.

People who fish must have perseverance, never become discouraged, and always be willing to try again. They must also have an "eye for the right moment"; they will know there are times when it is useless to fish—either the weather is wrong, the water is too murky, or the moon is in the wrong cycle.

They will use the right bait. I always wondered how my father knew exactly which bait to use at a particular spot. At times we would use crickets, earthworms, catalpa worms, fresh-water shrimp, or minnows. Through experience, he knew the kinds of fish in those areas and what they liked best.

Those who fish must also be very unobtrusive. They must be very quiet and keep themselves out of sight of the fish as much as possible. Sometimes one's shadow determines whether fish will bite.

Fishing in the day of Peter, Andrew, James, and John was really not much different from our methods today. No matter what method is used, effective fishers must be patient, persevering, sensitive to the right time, know the right bait, and keep themselves out of sight.

Jesus understood such things. He had grown up only a few miles from the Sea of Galilee. There is no question that he was steeped in the folklore and legend of the art of fishing. So it is not beyond our imagination to believe that he evaluated some of his very first disciples by such standards. We might even say that Christianity was first organized on that day when Jesus walked along the shores of the Sea of Galilee.

The first four disciples were fishermen, and three of those four—Peter, James, and John—became closest to Jesus of the original twelve. Having chosen these men because of their qualities, Jesus then gave them a mission: "Follow me, and I will make you fishers of men."

Our familiarity with this text might cause us to overlook its deeper meaning. There are two ideas involved. First, there is a period of preparation—"Follow me, and I will make . . . "; the verb used here is cast in the future tense. Second, there is the appointment to office itself—"make you fishers of men." The modern church commonly refers to that appointment as the task of evangelism.

We would do well to give serious consideration to both parts of this statement. Since Jesus recognized that these men had all the necessary qualities of good fishers of fish, he invited them to enter a period of preparation so as to translate those qualities into the qualities of good "fishers of men."

Of those qualities, patience is very important, since preaching and teaching and witnessing rarely experience quick results. They merely plant the seed; God gives the growth. And patience is very closely related to the matter of perseverance. The good teacher or preacher or witness must not be discouraged when nothing seems to happen. Some of the seeds we plant may not come up until long after we have departed this earth.

As to having an eye for the right time, common sense should tell us there are times when individuals will welcome the truth, but there are times when they resent the truth. When people are emotionally upset, unstable, or angry, they are not going to be open to suggestion. More often than not, the truth will harden their feelings. As the writer of Ecclesiastes reminds us, there is a time for every thing. Yes, a time to speak, and a time to be quiet.

And what about the right bait? I must confess I am not altogether comfortable with such terminology in connection with our tasks as evangelists for the Lord Jesus. *Bait* sounds as if we are involved in some scheme. Although we are not talking about gimmicks, we are dealing with human beings, and different individuals respond to different stimuli. Not all of us will be able to make a significant impact on all persons. This is a part of the patience we need to learn.

But what about the matter of the fisher (the evangelist) receding into the shadows? This is one of our most difficult tasks—to present Jesus Christ, not ourselves. I doubt seriously if any of us will ever succeed 100 percent, but at least we can try to help others focus on that figure beyond, not on us. That was the kind of preparation Jesus had in mind for his followers who were to be "fishers of men."

Over the years I have both preached on and listened to numerous sermons on this particular text. The task of evangelism is critical, and those sermonic efforts usually simply exhort all who have responded to Jesus Christ to assume the stance of "fishing"—that is, to become evangelists. I am not sure such an assumption is either valid or realistic.

We all know the overzealous and clumsy types who confront—and often affront—prospective converts. They succeed only in annoying. On the other hand, there are timid, indifferent church members who miss genuine opportunities for Christian witness. There is an old saying that 5 percent of the fishers catch 95 percent of the fish. That same ratio might apply to the church. It might be a mistake on our part to put too many lines into the water. Even as Jesus chose a small group for a very specific task, we need to prepare those of us who have skills in evangelism, and urge all others to choose supportive roles.

54

A supportive role is no less significant in the larger business of being fishers for Jesus Christ. Antonio Stradivari was the maker of the now priceless Stradivarius violins. An artist was critical of Antonio, saying he was just another craftsman—certainly less than an artist. In George Eliot's poem "Stradivarius," Antonio answers that artist:

> God be praised,
> Antonio Stradivari has an eye
> That winces at false work and loves the true . . .
> And for my fame—when any master holds
> 'Twixt chin and hand a violin of mine,
> He will be glad that Stradivari lived,
> Made violins, and made them of the best . . .
>
> I say not God Himself can make man's best
> Without best men to help Him . . .
>   'Tis God gives skill,
> But not without men's hands: He could not make
> Antonio Stradivari's violins
> Without Antonio.

Yes, we all have a part, and it matters not whether we are out front or behind the scenes. Every concern we express in behalf of this office of being "fishers of men" is a partial fulfillment of the call God has given us, and when we fail to fulfill this part of our calling, we do so at our own risk. We are responsible for the destiny of other human beings, just as we are responsible for our own. We cannot deal with one another with prejudice and emotion, but must deal with one another in the spirit of Jesus Christ.

I am quite sure I have failed to fulfill this office many times in my own life. I still cringe to recall an experience when I served as associate pastor thirty years ago. I had been asked by a distraught young wife to talk to her husband who was packing his bags to leave home. I pleaded with the man. I promised support. But he was adamant. He would not change his mind. Perhaps my immaturity caused me to become angry with him, but for all practical purposes the conversation ended with my telling him where to go. I have long since learned that I have been called to another task.

Jesus put no restrictions on those first fishermen. He ended his ministry upon this earth by giving the Great Commission: "Go into all the world . . . to all people." Our task of evangelism knows no limits. It simply awaits us to respond to his invitation: "Follow me, and I will make you fishers of men."

CHAPTER 6

Loyal Forever?

(The Solidarity of Discipleship)

John 6:55-69

The basic component of any group is loyalty. No club, business, country, team, or cause can survive without it. Loyalty is the lifeblood of corporate bodies.

Jesus needed it, too, but he had a hard time acquiring it. Things seemed encouraging at the outset of his ministry. He was, at first, an overnight sensation. Crowds gathered to hear him and followed him about. He was, as the rock musical expressed it a few years ago, *Jesus Christ, Superstar*. But it didn't last. Like snow in the spring, the crowds began to melt away. The Gospel of John states the blunt fact: "Many of his disciples drew back and no longer went about with him." Jesus was left with only a handful of disciples—the original twelve, plus a few more. And Jesus wondered about their solidarity, for he looked at them and asked, "Do you also wish to go away?"

Loyalty is one of the significant themes to which our attention is called on a regular basis. We sing about it and pray about it. We go out of

57

our way to make sure we are always recognized as true blue. We have no difficulty singing the words of the great old spiritual song: "Truehearted, wholehearted, faithful and loyal." I am not too apt at punctuation, but I have often wondered whether the writer should not have used a question mark, rather than an exclamation point, after the assertion, "Loyal forever." The first people who set out to follow Jesus had a problem with loyalty; are we that much different?

Loyalty is the willing devotion of a person to a cause, expressed in a sustained and practical manner. Perhaps the most familiar image has to do with a patriot's devotion to a country. In the August/September 1985 issue of *American Heritage*, there was a unique reference to this kind of loyalty. Interestingly, it did not concern American patriots, but Japanese patriots.

In August 1945, a large group of American ships entered Tokyo Bay two weeks after World War II had officially ended. The first ship behind the destroyers was the U.S.S. *San Diego*, under the command of Rear Admiral Oscar C. Badger. One of the communications officers on board the *San Diego* was Lieutenant Vernon C. Squires. Over the next several days Squires wrote two lengthy letters to his wife concerning his impressions and experiences. Those two letters were included in the article.

I was fascinated by Squires' description of the attitude of the Japanese people. It was felt there might still be some armed resistance, but amazingly, they found no opposition, either organized or unorganized. On the contrary, the people were so polite and courteous that most of the Americans were confused. On one trip into Tokyo, Squires and one of his fellow officers talked with a silk merchant who spoke fluent English.

Squires asked, "What's the explanation for this apparent lack of hostility or resentment among the Japanese toward the Americans?"

The merchant, somewhat perplexed, answered, "Why should there be any resentment now? We are defeated. We accept the situation always."

But that did not satisfy Squires. He reminded the merchant that less than a month before, the two nations had been at war.

The merchant answered, "Yes, to be sure. But now the emperor has ordered that all that be forgotten. Japanese are a very disciplined people. When the emperor tells us, we change our minds" ("Landing at Tokyo Bay," p. 24).

That is loyalty—devotion to a cause, expressed in a practical and sustained manner!

In his autobiography *River of Years*, Joseph Fort Newton maintains there are four things people can do with their lives. First, an individual can seek to run away from life and its responsibilities. That, of course, is what Jonah did. Second, one can run along with life, hunt with the pack and think with the herd—Everybody's doing it, why shouldn't I? Third, one can take hold of life with a singleness of purpose, submit to discipline, and run to some end. Or, fourth, one can give oneself up to a cause or purpose and let that cause or purpose control one's life.

In all probability, the majority of people today would fall into the second category. These are the individuals who run along with life, always adapting to their environment, taking on the complexion of their society. They are the "moldees" of a society, not the "molders" ([Lippincott, 1946], p. 312).

One of the most significant acts any of us can perform is to choose the right yardstick by which to measure our life. And there is no better yardstick than our loyalty.

Some governments still try to gain people's allegiance with loyalty oaths, but such attempts are merely carryovers from the feudal age when serfs were required to swear fealty to their lords. That is not true loyalty. Jesus understood that, so he asked only whether it was the disciples' intention to stay, or to separate themselves. He knew true loyalty springs from the union of natural interest and free choice.

Loyalty cannot be created by compulsion or by a commitment with a built-in escape hatch. Some of our modern ideas about marriage illustrate this point well. Since the first stirrings of what oddly has been termed the New Morality, many otherwise thoughtful people have argued that living together without marriage might not be such a bad thing after all. Without the "piece of paper" that made their marriage legal, couples could test their "sexual compatibility" and "get in touch with their feelings," realizing that if these things did not work out, they could dissolve the agreement and no one would be the worse for the experiment.

Yes, that sounded pretty good, but it did not work out as many had hoped. In the past fifteen years, divorces, broken homes, sexual confusion, and unwanted children have, as statistics show, increased at about the same rate as the popularity of cohabitation. The solution apparently became the problem.

According to one marriage manual, couples should marry only when they have a self-giving Christian love, one that is ready for sacrifice. It should be like the love of Christ for his spouse, the Church.

Perhaps Jesus, even in the first century, knew that human loyalties are not always fixed in a covenant relationship. The early crowds that flocked to hear him, but bailed out when the demands for discipleship were clearly enunciated, were not unlike the disciples of the New Morality and their attitude toward the marriage commitment. Loyalty cannot be demanded. But when it becomes our natural choice, made with the strongest commitment we can give it, it is a thing of beauty (*Pulpit Resources* 13/3:29).

Loyalty is the pathway to solving the problem of the purpose of life. Our true good can be won only outside ourselves, in self-surrender to God. God made us so that our own wills are by nature restless until they rest in harmony with

God's will. As Josiah Royce expressed it in his classic *Philosophy of Loyalty*, "Loyalty is the Will to Believe in something eternal, and to express that belief in the practical life of a human being" (Hackett Publishing Co., 1982; Macmillan, 1908).

Thomas Naylor is a professor of economics at Duke University. In an address at his home church in Durham, North Carolina, he expressed his thoughts after an extended visit to the Soviet Union and Hungary. He feels there is good news from those countries, on both the economic and the religious front. For one thing, religion is thriving.

However, there is also some bad news—not only from Russia but from the United States as well. We are dealing with a common enemy that can be cured by neither capitalism nor communism. That common enemy is a lack of meaning in our lives, a spiritual emptiness, godlessness.

Naylor teaches courses in corporate strategy to students twenty-five to forty years of age. He once asked each student to submit a ten-year personal strategic plan reflecting goals and objectives upon completing the work at Duke. With very few exceptions, the students were interested in money, power, and things—very big things. No mention was made of personal or spiritual growth, and only token interest was expressed in family. By their own admission these students felt a sense of emptiness in their lives which they felt money and power and things could fill. This is godlessness American-style.

While in the Soviet Union, Naylor met

numerous professionals in that same age range. For the most part they seemed pragmatic and nonideological. They were interested in jogging, aerobics, television, designer blue jeans, fancy automobiles. Indeed, their value system seemed dangerously close to that of American yuppies. They too suffer from a lack of meaning in their lives, caused in part by their risk-free society— they are guaranteed jobs, low-cost flats, free education and medical care, and inexpensive public transportation.

The younger generation of Russians seeks to cope with this meaninglessness in a variety of ways, including excessive consumption of alcohol and tobacco. They also search for meaning through the restoration of old buildings, palaces, and churches. Dr. Naylor believes that Soviet leaders are showing increased tolerance for organized religion because, deep down, they know the church is fulfilling a need the state cannot possibly fulfill.

Outside our basic interest in the tension that exists between the two superpowers of this earth, we need to ask, What does this dilemma say to us? It tells us that the answer to our emptiness grows out of the loyalty we are capable of giving to our Lord Jesus Christ.

We stand at a critical crossroad, and we must determine in which direction we shall travel. Our spirits are haunted by our Lord's question, "Do you also wish to go away?" Let us answer with resolve, "Lord, to whom shall we go? You have the words of eternal life!"

CHAPTER 7

In a Time of Tension— Fear Haunts!

(The Seriousness of Discipleship)

Luke 13:31-35

We are all familiar with the children's story of *Jack and the Beanstalk.* Jack planted some beans and one stalk grew so high it touched the sky. Jack climbed the beanstalk and in the clouds, discovered a giant's castle. As Jack inspected the castle, he felt the ground beneath him tremble, and he heard a loud voice saying, "Fee, fie, fo, fum. I smell the blood of an Englishman!" The giant chased Jack, but Jack slipped away, slid down the beanstalk, and chopped the whole thing down, killing the giant. Everyone had thought Jack a dull, foolish lad, but now he became known as Jack the Giant Killer.

We need that story today, for there are giants on the prowl in our land—angry giants, evil giants, giants that would eat us alive. And what is even worse, there seems to be a great scarcity of heroes. We question why there were so few individuals of strong character available for the presidency of our country, particularly when we contrast the present situation with the past. Today the ground still shakes at the nearness of giants. We still hear their bestial "Fee, fie, fo, fum!" and, like Jack, we fear and run and hide. But all too often, unlike Jack, we never slay the giants.

Our Scripture from the Gospel of Luke tells the same kind of story. But the incident recorded there was not a fairy tale. It actually happened. Herod, a giant of his day, and Jesus, a simple carpenter turned itinerant preacher, faced each other in the harsh world of reality. At first glance, it seems a gross mismatch—Herod, the rich, armed man of authority, against Jesus, the quiet, small-town preacher with no army, no power, no money.

There is no question that our Lord had numerous enemies. From his birth, there were those who plotted to take his life. However, Herod represented the most formidable. At a time when Jesus was steadfastly turning his face toward Jerusalem, he found himself on Herod's hit list.

In *The Gospel of Luke*, William Barclay points out a most interesting thought when he reminds us that not all Pharisees were hostile to Jesus. There were those who actually warned him he was in danger and advised him to seek safety (Westminster Press, 1977).

Common sense should tell us that we cannot make blanket indictments of groups of people. One of the flaws in our human fabric is that we jump to conclusions; we tend to lump everyone who goes by a certain name or title into one mind-set. Even the Jews of Jesus' day knew there were good and bad Pharisees. There may have been six bad ones for every good one, but it is clear that there were Pharisees who admired and respected Jesus.

We are not told their motivation. We can only surmise their reason for giving him this warning. It is clear they must have had great fear of Herod. And, we must add, there was basic substance to that fear. They remembered the fate of John the Baptist. They knew Herod need not account for such actions to Rome. As long as he kept down insurrection and revolution, Rome did not bother him. Indeed, he kept possible insurrection down through execution. Throughout the ages, tyrants and dictators have ruled by fear.

But Jesus was not intimidated by Herod's threats. He directly confronted whatever fear he might have had. In calling Herod a fox, he compared him to an animal noted for its deceptiveness. There is no question that Jesus knew his enemy. He knew Herod was an adulterer living with his brother's wife. And he knew Herod was a wicked despot who would stop at nothing to secure his throne.

Who is the Herod in your life? What giant is threatening you? Is it another human being, a person in a position of authority? Or is that giant not a "someone"? Is it a "something"? Could it be pornography, the drug traffic, theological secularism, the ecological crisis? Or is it possible that the giant threatening you is old age?

Some time ago I received an anonymous

letter, a poignant expression of the fears and frustrations of old age: "Pastor, as long as one is young, vital to a busy world, everything seems rosy and okay; but when one loses their good health and gets old, it makes a different story." I was impressed by the closing of the letter, for it was signed, "Alone, but not lonely—for He has promised me, 'Lo, I am with you always' . . . and always means eternity!" Old age is a giant that freezes many individuals into a sense of uselessness and hopelessness.

Like Jesus, we need to confront our fears. If we try to hide from them, they will pursue us. But if we confront them, you can begin to handle them.

Remember the story of Sleepy Hollow? In Washington Irving's legend, Ichabod Crane, a schoolteacher, was wooing the belle of a small New England community. His rival for her love was a younger man. Now, in that community there was a legend about a headless horseman who rode around the countryside at night. Ichabod's love rival dressed up as the headless phantom and, late one night, lay in wait for Ichabod. As Ichabod rode by, the headless horseman gave pursuit. Poor Ichabod was so frightened he spurred his horse and was never seen again. If only he had turned to confront his fears, he would have discovered they were harmless.

What do you do when you are afraid? How do you respond to a threat? Do you give up and cry? Do you run away? Do you ignore it? Or, like Jesus, do you stand up and confront your fear?

The text tells us that Jesus faced Herod. It also tells us he did so with courage. Jesus knew all too well that Herod could make good his threats. But he did not accept the advice of the Pharisees. He stood up to Herod!

This is a word the church needs to hear today. The church has many enemies: the creeping secularism of minds, the sensationalism of the mass media, the social acceptability of drugs and alcohol, and on and on we could go. We have run from these destructive giants too long. The church is like a mighty army with the soldiers asleep in their tents. As a pastor, I identify with that general who said, "I wish I had as many soldiers as I have men."

Shortly after the capitulation of France in World War II, Winston Churchill called a cabinet meeting and outlined the grave situation that confronted them. Quite literally, England stood alone against Germany's war machine. The faces of the cabinet members registered deep despair. Churchill himself was silent for a few moments; then he smiled and said, "Gentlemen, I find it rather inspiring."

Do you have any spark of that kind of courage? Others have. We see it in young David as he took up his slingshot and went to face Goliath. We see it in Jesus as he faced Herod the fox. It was there in Martin Luther when he faced the church courts.

It was present in the incomparable Hugh Latimer, the first great English preacher of social righteousness. Once when Latimer was preaching in Westminster Abbey, King Henry was present. Bishop Latimer soliloquized, "Latimer! Latimer! Latimer! Be careful what you say. The king of England is here!" Then he added, "Latimer! Latimer! Latimer! Be careful what you say. The King of Kings is here" (Barclay, *Gospel of Luke*, p. 186).

But where are the Latimers, the Davids, the Luthers, the Wesleys, today? Are you such a one? Will you stand up to your fears with a godly courage?

Confrontation. Courage. These are ways the Lord Jesus Christ dealt with fear. He continued with his normal ministry. He refused to quit or become preoccupied with worry. He said, "Go and tell that fox, 'Behold, I cast out demons and perform cures today and tomorrow, and the third day I finish my course. Nevertheless I must go on my way today and tomorrow and the day following.' "

Each of us well knows the temptation to quit. We know how to worry. We have seen worry and fear become a neurotic complex. Jesus did not allow this to happen. He knew full well that Herod might take off his head. But he also knew that God was with him; he had a mission to carry out.

There is a stimulating analogy to Jesus' situation recorded in the Old Testament. The prophet Nehemiah felt called of God to rebuild the walls around the city of Jerusalem. He believed this would return the city to its former greatness. But his enemies discouraged him. His work was constantly hassled, and he was threatened with death. But Nehemiah knew the work must go on, and go on it did, though he held a sword in one hand and a trowel in the other.

What a symbol that is for the church in any age. Tragically, we still have the hecklers in our midst. There are those who want us to fight among ourselves, even those who would destroy us. If we must work with a sword in one hand and a trowel in the other, so be it. The work must go on!

We Christians are like white corpuscles in the blood stream. We go wherever we are needed to fight infection. We scatter throughout the world to bring conversion, healing, reform, justice. And it is a continuous job!

Someone once said, "Patriotism is not a short, frenzied outburst of emotion but the tranquil and steady dedication of a lifetime." Faithfulness to God is the very same. It is not a month-long quest of emotional zeal. It is the patient plodding of a lifetime. I mean this quite literally. Faithfulness is a lifetime struggle.

In the "Peanuts" comic strip, Charlie Brown quizzes Linus, "What if everyone was like you? What if we all ran away from our problems? . . . What if everyone in the whole world suddenly decided to run away from his problems?"

71

Linus replies, "Well, at least we'd all be running in the same direction!"

Poor Linus! With that kind of attitude he will never be a Jack the Giant Killer. He will be only an Ichabod Crane. Shakespeare once wrote, "The coward dies a thousand deaths."

What about you? Will you die a thousand deaths, fleeing shadows and cowering in your hiding place? Or will you come out fighting?

CHAPTER 8

Who Has the Power?
Who Is in Control?

(The Surrender of Discipleship)

Psalm 145:8-13

Toward the end of Jesus' earthly ministry, he was arrested and brought before Pontius Pilate. The contrast between Pilate and Jesus seems devastating. Pilate is in control. Jesus, on the other hand, appears powerless. His hands securely fastened, his disciples scattered and bewildered, he stands alone.

Pilate seeks an easy way out by urging Jesus to confess he is a king. That would be grounds enough to make the charges stick.

But this is where appearances can be deceiving. Pilate may have been in control, but Jesus had the power. To attain atonement for our sins he had given up control, but he had the power of God, and that power was realized according to God's plan.

The questions, Who has the power? Who is in control? become the basic elements in most human relationships. It is human nature to want both power and control over events in our lives. Or to put it more succinctly, we are never more vulnerable than when we are rendered powerless

73

and when control has been taken from us. Power and control are two very significant issues which require our best Christian response.

We can illustrate the difference between power and control by remembering an event that took place in rural Tennessee. An escaped convict with a drawn gun surprised a woman who was cooking breakfast. Amazingly, she was not afraid of the gun. This small, grandmotherly woman told the convict to put his gun down while she fixed him some breakfast. She spoke of her faith and instructed the young man in the way he should behave. In no time at all, that young man had surrendered and was on his way back to prison.

That young man had the gun. He thought he was in control. But he had not reckoned with the power of a woman who was not intimidated. Power is always greater than control. Indeed, mature people realize that the goal in life is not control, but power.

This does not mean that the concept of control is totally evil. Common sense tells us there must be a sense of control; otherwise we would be victimized by an arbitrary anarchy in which everyone claimed control but no one actually had it.

However, one who is concerned only about control is destined for total frustration, if not destruction. Many believe this is a problem of governments today; they formulate foreign policy on the concept of control rather than power. Some say our nation is attempting to control Central and Latin America with guns, warships, embargoes, and covert activity. They believe it would be much better if we used the power of freedom, goodwill, democracy, and understanding to do the job.

History teaches us that governments that rule through control do not last. Why is it that our government, based upon the Constitution, is now one of the oldest on the face of the earth? It is because the Constitution was based upon power rather than upon control.

Of course, human lives also operate on this principle. Parents must exercise some control over young children. They would be rather irresponsible if they did not keep their children away from heaters and staircases. However, once these lessons are learned, it is necessary for children to experience their parents' power rather than their control—the power of love, mutual respect, and trust.

Of the mistakes we parents make, the most basic is that we lean much more toward control than toward power. Control does not encourage a child's self-trust or self-respect.

Our human lives, at any age, are very complex, but why is it that some children are not devastated when confronted with their violation of a rule? Is it simply that their temperaments are different from those of other children? Not really! The ultimate difference has to do with the management concept of the parents—do they control, or are they basing their relationship upon power? Show me a child who has become increasingly aware that no matter what happens, he or she is still loved, and I will show you a child who can be reprimanded.

Over the years, I have dealt with many children and youths. I remember a young woman who was a college freshman. She was a very attractive, but a very unhappy young woman, bordering on severe depression. As we tried to untangle some of the heartache she had known, it became apparent that her basic problem grew out of a conflict with her mother. On the surface, the two were perhaps closer than most mothers and daughters. Great mutual love was professed. However, that mother's love was the most possessive I can remember. Such love can be terribly destructive. Although most of us never intend this to happen, the conflict arises out of our lack of faith in power and our overwhelming desire for control.

But even here we become confused, for Scripture teaches us that as human beings, we have no power of our own. An engineer might permit a small child to throw a switch and thereby activate power that does not belong to the child. In the same way, through prayer, God permits us to turn the switch, so to speak, and receive his energy. Then we are vessels through which power surges, but that power is not our own.

Our human nature leans strongly toward a desire for both power and control, but we should be very careful about the way we seek them. In fact, we should ultimately shun the concept of control. That leaves us with power, and if we have no power that truly belongs to us, how can we hope to cope?

First, let me suggest that we examine the power available to us. It is divine power, the power of God, the omnipotence of God. In the words of the psalmist,

> The LORD is faithful in all his words,
> and gracious in all his deeds.
> The LORD upholds all who are falling,
> and raises up all who are bowed down.
>   (Psalm 145:13c-14)

The psalmist is especially anxious for us to understand that God's omnipotence is about power, not control. That is a lesson we people of faith have been slow to learn. We have assumed that omnipotence—the possession of unlimited power or authority—means God has both power and control. God is all-power. But God has chosen to surrender control by granting us free choice. From the time of Adam and Eve, God has exercised little if any control over human beings.

Many of us become confused by the questions, Why do bad things happen to good people? and Why does God allow sickness and natural calamity? Our frustration grows out of our belief that God controls human destinies. If that were so, we would have no responsibility and therefore would not be under judgment for our irresponsibility. God does, however, give us the power to endure and surmount. And that power will eventually triumph.

The gospel invites us to come face to face with a Savior who gave up control and thereby unleashed a force that still changes lives today. His self-surrender—turning the other cheek, loving enemies, submitting to Roman soldiers— shows he wanted no control. Instead, he allowed Divine Power to flow through his life and today we have a two-thousand-year record of this success.

What does this mean? It means we do not need to ricochet from pillar to post, worrying about whether we have power or control. God has promised that his power is available to us; we must have the faith to use it.

That, of course, is where our problem lies. Because we have been brainwashed to believe we must be in control, we can never humble ourselves to accept the power God has promised us. But nobody can do it for us! That power means nothing unless we have the faith to accept it and use it. Otherwise, we experience only emptiness. Are you willing to learn from those who have gone before? Are you willing to let the witness of the ages speak to you?

God has thrown in his lot with the ultimate powerlessness of human existence. He permits us to participate in his world-conquering power, which manifests itself in faith, hope, and love.

Charles Schulz, the creator of "Peanuts,"

describes how he discovered and experienced this power:

I grew up an only child, and my mother died the very week I was drafted. . . . Before going into the Armed Forces I met a minister of the Church of God. . . . He walked into my father's barbershop one day in St. Paul, Minnesota. . . . It was not long after that that we called upon him to preach my mother's funeral sermon. After coming back from the Army, I began to attend services at his little church. We had an active group of young people—all of us were in our twenties—and we began studying the Bible together. The more I thought about the matter during those study times, the more I realized that I really loved God. I recognized the fact that he had pulled me through a depression in which I had been torn apart from everything I knew, and that he had enabled me to survive so many experiences. ("Knowing You Are Not Alone," *Decision* 4[September 1963]:9)

In the past few years we have heard a great deal about alternate sources of fuel and power. There is a basic belief that when we can harness the power of the sun, our problems will be over.

But we do have available now the power of God's Son, Jesus Christ. We do not need to wait. To receive that power, we simply need the faith to surrender our desire for control.

CHAPTER 9

Before Your Ship Comes in, It Must First Go Out!

(The Subordination of Discipleship)

II Thessalonians 3:6-13

I heard a woman describe a fairly familiar sight in a New York subway, or anywhere vending machines are placed. A small boy walked the whole length of the subway platform, pushing the plungers of all the machines. He hoped that by some miracle he could get a piece of gum or candy without putting in a coin, that perhaps one of the machines might be out of order.

Many people are like that. Just as the little boy went along the subway platform, they go through life, making futile attempts to get something for nothing, to receive some prize without putting in any true effort. From time to time I find myself talking about something I will do "when my ship comes in." But then I always remember I have never sent a ship out.

Our Scripture lesson contains Paul's strong rebuke of the Christians in Thessalonica. They were so excited by the expected second coming of Christ, many had quit their jobs and abandond the normal routines of life, expecting to be supported by the church. And they urged others to join them.

Paul emphasized the role of work, denounced idleness, and scolded the freeloaders. Those who did not supply bread should not eat, he said. "For you yourselves know how you ought to imitate us; we were not idle when we were with you, we did not eat anyone's bread without paying, but with toil and labor we worked night and day, that we might not burden any of you." The Thessalonians had forgotten that the best way to prepare for Christ's coming is to be active and diligent in the discharge of daily work and duty.

Paul was right, but we should not blindly champion work. There are times when we need to be somewhat wary of it. More specifically, we should be careful when it interferes with things of the spirit.

When Jesus visited the home of Mary and Martha in the little village of Bethany, Martha wanted to make sure every little detail was cared for so that nothing could go wrong while the eminent visitor was present. But Jesus chided Martha. She could have found rest for her spirit if she had not been such a slave to work.

Rather than being an instrument for the sustaining of our lives, work sometimes becomes a fetish, an idol we worship. Or the very opposite can happen. We can become so indifferent to work that we become spongers. This is not intended as an antiwelfare statement. A program of public assistance for those who cannot help themselves is one of the distinguishing marks of civilization. It is nothing short of cruel to deny a helping hand to the elderly, disabled, infirm, and those who genuinely want to work but cannot find employment.

No, this is a very straightforward admonition to the unemployed in this country who choose not to work. These people live off of one kind of hustle or another—food stamps, unemployment payments, welfare programs. Some complain they cannot find "meaningful" work. They are the takers rather than the suppliers. The consequence is a sad waste, chiefly of their own lives.

On August 17, 1981, *The New York Times* reported a scene in Cambodia where an international hunger-relief organization was distributing food. "Hundreds of people waited quietly for their share, but when fishnets were handed out, the people cheered." A large part of our population might learn a "meaningful" lesson from our Cambodian brothers and sisters.

Paul was not emphasizing any of the extremes represented here. His point was, Earn your own way. Don't be a parasite, a goldbrick, a loafer, a drone who can but won't make its own way. Pull your own weight, earn your keep, don't be a burden on others.

When Paul described the Thessalonians as being idle, the Greek word he used is a miliatry term meaning *insubordination*. It generally refers to a violation of military discipline, especially that of a soldier who breaks ranks in battle. Since Christian discipleship is often compared to a military campaign, we have no difficulty in applying that analogy to our own lives. Christians are not to be undisciplined soldiers who cannot be counted upon to stand fast in the thick of battle against the forces of evil. We must not be guilty of disorderly conduct.

Another meaning of that Greek word is *truancy*. The same word is found in a contract dated A.D. 66, in which a father apprenticed his son to a weaver. The father was obligated to feed and clothe the boy, while the weaver provided his pocket money. If, however, the son was truant during the year, it was up to the father to see that the missing days were made up. The Thessalonian Christians were *truant* in their Christian duty. Christians are not to behave like children who skip school.

Perhaps you saw the segment on the NBC Saturday evening news in October 1984, concerning the work of a truant officer in Cleveland, Ohio. Sadly, it was noted that each day, more than two thousand young people skipped school. Most of them congregated in video arcades. A large number skipped school regularly without their parents' knowledge. Paul says this attitude on the part of a Christian is destructive, irresponsible, an insult to the faith itself.

That truancy, that lack of discipline, poses perhaps the greatest temptation for most nominal Christians. Far more sweeping than the refusal to work for a living, it includes all aspects of the

Christian life: general moral conduct, regularity of prayer and worship, consistent performance of good works, and the active evangelism that begins with the general impression we make upon the world.

Such truancy from daily Christian life is so serious that Paul issued a command in the name of Christ. Those of the congregation who were not guilty of insubordination to the discipline of the Christian life were to express their disapproval of those who were. Imagine the repercussions in the church today if such a command were to be given!

Paul is not calling for such persons to be excommunicated. They are still to be thought of as brothers and sisters, but since they pose a danger to the church, they are to be avoided lest they infect others. Yes, I can imagine the great outcry such a command would bring today. But the sad truth is that the disciplined, committed individuals do not need to ostracize the truants. They have done that to themselves!

One of the striking differences between the Christian and other religions is their attitude toward work. Buddha is usually portrayed as seated and meditating. And the gods of ancient Greece and Rome were thought to dwell at ease on Mount Olympus, relishing ambrosia and nectar. A number of world religions have made virtues of idleness or repose.

Contrast that, however, with the attitude of the Christian faith. Jesus said, "My Father is working still, and I am working" (John 5:17).

85

Nothing rings of laziness there. In creation God worked and, in contemplating that work, declared it to be very good. It is sometimes supposed that work is a curse that came upon Adam and Eve because of their sin. This is a mistaken notion. Man had been given the work assignment before the Fall, when he was commanded to settle the earth and subdue it, to have dominion over all creation.

The Bible holds work in high esteem. Abel was a shepherd. Noah built a great ship. The Patriarchs were herdsmen. Moses tended sheep. David came from the fields. Many of the prophets worked with their hands. Jesus called some of his disciples from the sea and the marketplace. Paul was a tent maker. And was not Jesus himself a carpenter?

Though the apostle Paul was dealing with a particular situation in Thessalonica, he was citing a general principle—Christians are not excused from their human and religious commitments on the pretext that nothing matters in the long run.

Our circumstance today is not too unlike that in Thessalonica. Many individuals have forsaken their religious commitments—not because they are enthusiastically looking forward to the triumphant return of Jesus Christ, but because they have become skeptical concerning the value of anything we, as humans, do in this world. What does it matter? Evil is stronger than good, the world will be blown to bits by some nuclear holocaust anyway, and nobody else seems to care!

It is this kind of pessimism, both real and imagined, that Christians are called upon to avoid today, for such attitudes can infect the body of Christ and have, in instances, made it sick even to the point of death.

Gabriel Fackre, in *Word in Deed*, has suggested a unique metaphor for the people of God. We are to function as "dawn people." It is only then that we can be and do so that we have the time of our lives and, indeed, announce with power "the Day of the Lord." Fackre tells a story which he insists is the basic thread running throughout the Bible. "God had a dream. It was a vision of a world together." He goes on to say that this divine intention might be described as a lively campfire. God is the roaring blaze. Humanity is a circle of celebrative dancers, arms linked, facing one another and the light ([Eerdmans, 1975], chap. 2).

What is our basic life-style as modern-day disciples of Jesus Christ? Do we see ourselves as "dawn people" who gladly link arms with others and celebrate about a great campfire? Or are we like those slothful Thessalonians whose insubordination not only was destroying themselves, but was infecting the rest of the church? We had best answer that!

CHAPTER 10

Security—Social or Spiritual?

(The Security of Discipleship)

Ephesians 6:10-20

Our youngest daughter was married recently and though she received lovely and thoughtful gifts, one was missing. It was a gift she had been promised and actually would not have been a gift at all, because it had been hers when she was very small. It was her "yum-yum." To be more specific, it was her baby blanket. Like Linus in the comic strip "Peanuts," she had a security blanket. One of our friends persuaded her to give up her yum-yum when she was two years old with the promise that when she married it would be returned.

Everybody has a yum-yum, a source of security. Some individuals believe that all of life is a quest for security. Insurance, burglar alarms, health foods, karate courses, safety belts—these are but a few of our defenses against things we believe threaten our security.

Some people seek a sense of safety by clinging to a traditional role, mistrusting anything that represents change. Others turn to dogmatism and cults. A growing number look for security in addiction: Millions are enslaved to cigarettes, pills, alcohol, drugs, even food. And there are those who look for safety in star images, television, work, and immature behavior.

Some women who have suffered deep emotional injury in love or marriage may vow never to let another man control their emotions; they thus find security in the role of the hard and bitter spinster. More common are the sensitive young men who learn to encrust themselves in a "tough guy" shell, or those who brag to cover feelings of inadequacy.

In spite of such substitutes, the human need for security, and our search for it, are legitimate. Centuries ago the psalmist found security in the Lord:

> I lift up my eyes to the hills.
>   From whence does my help come?
> My help comes from the LORD,
>   who made heaven and earth. (Psalm 121:1-2)

There follows a litany, telling how the Lord will "keep" one who trusts in him. *Keep* is a secure word. It conveys the concept of being protected.

The passage in Ephesians provides a similar metaphor: The believer can find security in "the whole armor of God." Our security rests not in our efforts to fortify ourselves against life's hazards, but in our surrender to God. Our own arsenals of protection are inadequate compared to the "armor of God."

Frederick Buechner reflects on the purpose of

SECURITY—SOCIAL OR SPIRITUAL?

that armor in a sermon entitled "The Two Battles" (*Magnificent Defeat* [Seabury Press, 1966]). He says the battle most individuals consider of greatest importance is the battle to get ahead. If that is true, what Paul describes as the armor of God will weigh us down, even render us more vulnerable. But what if the battle to get ahead is not the most important thing? What if that "other" war—the war to become a human being, to become whole and at peace within ourselves—is most important? If that is the case, then the "whole armor of God" is not an encumbrance, but an enabler. It causes life to open up, and that is security!

Our problem is one of choice. We listen to the ancient words of the Apostle. He talks about principalities and powers. He speaks of the wiles of the devil. He uses that awful word *defiled* as if it were some stain on the soul or a spiritual virus. To our modern ears, the language of Scripture sounds bizarre or ridiculous or downright superstitious. Surely it has nothing to do with our everyday situations. We moderns have long since done away with irrational fears of spooky forces and spiritual pollution. We know the issue is choice, not contact. Or do we? I am not at all sure we know that as well as we should.

Down deep, most of us, regardless of age, are still wrestling with the fear into which we were born. Our desire for security begins at the moment of birth. From conception until we are born, our every desire and wish is satisfied. A fetus has no worry and can have none, since its only contact is with a constant surrounding.

The newborn baby is in for a rude awakening. Its security system is left behind. It must learn to breathe for itself and put up with the inconsistencies of life that will bombard it until the day it dies. It is stated succinctly by Paul and Mark Keller: "We are born into fear because we are separated." They make the point that in spite of our strong survival instincts, we are disposed toward self-destruction, and we reach for control out of fear (*Kairios Sermon Aid Table Talks* [July-September 1985]:19-20).

Viktor Frankl, in *The Unheard Cry for Meaning*, says that someone who worries about "the meaning of life is proving his humanness. . . . The search for meaning [and that, of course, is another way of saying *security*] is a distinctive characteristic of being human. No other animal has ever cared whether there is a meaning to life" ([Simon & Schuster, 1978], pp. 28-29).

That's an interesting observation, isn't it? We live out our lives, not in some empty vacuum, but in a day-by-day struggle. We wrestle with whether to yield our lives out of fear to some control we are not sure we trust, or to risk ourselves to some eternal promise. Which makes more sense? We know which is easier—that is, which does not demand as much from us individually. But that is not the issue.

Think about the birth process. After birth an infant is exposed to a second security system—the mother's arms, the sheltering house, the comforting cradle—and finds a certain security in these containments. Slowly the small child learns to feel safe in ever more open spaces, ever more complex patterns.

But remember, that child never ceases to need the rhythmic, restorative return to what is easy, familiar, trusted. After its first tentative steps, it will plop down on its bottom, a return to the security of the familiar.

How alive would we be if we were to discover some perfect Camelot where all our needs would be automatically met? We might feel safe, but would we be satisfied? I really doubt it. Risk and adventure constitute the very essence of our existence.

What hope would there be for business if individuals were unwilling to risk their time and money simply because they might fail? What hope is there for students if they consistently refuse to form an opinion on any subject because they might be wrong? Security grows out of an increasing ability to cope with both success and failure, out of living not in an insulated society but in a world of challenge.

To put it more succinctly, who feels more secure than those who will not cower and lose courage in the midst of danger? Who are more free in spirit than those who know that no matter how severe their suffering, they will not be deterred from doing their best in the face of evil?

The essential nature of our human struggle is inward, and by ourselves, we cannot win the day. That is the real thrust of Paul's message to the Ephesian Christians. "Be strong in the Lord" becomes more than a rallying point; it becomes a way of life. It represents the source of security that gives us strength and courage.

These words represent Paul's parting thoughts to a group of persons with whom he has been deeply involved for several years. He loves them as a parent loves an infant. He is protective of them and very much aware of the intensity of the struggle before them. I do not know whether life was more terrifying for people of the first century. I do know that people in that ancient time believed implicitly in evil spirits, which filled the air and were always at work to do human beings harm. That is the meaning of terms such as "principalities and powers" and "wiles of the devil."

You and I may use different language, but the experience has not changed. It is reported that Robert Louis Stevenson once said, "You know the Caledonian Railway Station in Edinburgh? One cold, east windy morning, I met Satan there." We do not know exactly what happened to Stevenson that morning, but we recognize the experience. All of us at times have felt the effect of evil. Sometimes it is the icy grip of guilt. At other times it results when the juice of life has been squeezed from us. What do we do in such circumstance? Is there any security?

Here is Scripture's answer: "Be strong in the Lord!" Then those unique weapons of the whole armor of God begin to make some sense. What are those weapons?—truth, righteousness, faith, peace, salvation. If we do not find security in such weapons, where will we find it? At times our reputations, our money, our ability to talk our way out of any kind of trap may help us, but not when our lives are out there on the very cutting edge of the battle line.

One of the great theologians of the twentieth century, Karl Barth, confessed to a recurring dream. He saw himself arriving at the pearly gates pulling a child's red wagon, in which were stacked all his writings. He believed the dream was telling him that in the final analysis, all his theologizing was mere child's play compared to God's great grace. All that he was and hoped to be depended upon one thing—God's grace.

That is our security: "Be strong in the Lord!"

CHAPTER 11

A Way out of Hell

(The Salvation of Discipleship)

Deuteronomy 30:15-20

In one of the closing scenes of the award-winning movie *Gandhi,* a Hindu leader came to the bedside of Gandhi to plead that he end his long fast. Gandhi reaffirmed that he would partake of food only when the Hindus and Moslems ceased fighting. The Hindu, with hatred in his eyes, stated that he would continue to fight. To justify his resolve, he told Gandhi that Moslems had killed his little boy by crushing his head. He in turn, had captured a Moslem boy and killed him the same way.

Then he added sorrowfully, "I have been living in hell."

Gandhi reflected for a few moments. Then he said softly, "I think I know a way out of hell." With the Hindu hanging on his words, Gandhi told him to find a boy similar to the son the Moslems had killed, take him into his home, and raise him as a Moslem. Mahatma Gandhi was a Hindu, but he articulated the noblest teaching of Jesus Christ—overcome evil with good.

Gandhi was reiterating that age-old text from

the book of Deuteronomy—Choose Life! He was telling that bitter Hindu leader what the Lord God Almighty has been telling his people through the ages: Choose life over death . . . choose heaven over hell. Decide on a life of blessing over a life that is a curse. That is the message of our text: "I have set before you life and death, blessing and curse; therefore choose life, that you and your descendants may live" (vs. 19).

Life is the one big choice everyone has. We do not choose to be born. We do not choose our parents. We do not choose our historical epoch, the country of our birth, or the color of our skin. We have little to say about our upbringing. Nor do most of us choose the time and circumstances of our death.

But we do choose how we shall live—courageously or in cowardice, honorably or dishonorably, with purpose or adrift. We decide what is important and what is trivial. We decide what we do and what we refuse to do. We decide. We choose. And as we decide and choose, so are our lives formed.

I believe one of the first steps young people take toward becoming responsible persons is their acceptance of the fact that they have a choice, that they are not victims of evil conspiracies. In other words, it is not what happens to us, but what we are that makes a difference, and we choose what we will be. No one else chooses. We make that determination ourselves.

We can imagine Moses standing before the

people of Israel, chiding and challenging them to make the right decision—a decision that will affect their destiny. He reminds them that while they were slaves in Egypt they had no set of alternatives and therefore choice was neither required nor possible. Now, however, God has delivered them out of Egypt and through the wilderness, and they now stand poised, ready to possess a land as their own.

But that was not all. At Mount Sinai they had entered into a covenant with God. They had been instructed in God's law so they would understand the two options now available to them: They could be the people of God, or they could be just another secular nation among the nations of the world. Before them in one direction lies God's road into the land of Canaan; in another direction lies the way of the world into the land. The choice they make will be the determining factor.

In Lewis Carroll's delightful *Alice in Wonderland*, Alice was following a path through a forest when it divided. Standing irresolute, Alice inquired of the Cheshire Cat, who suddenly had appeared in a nearby tree, which path she should take.

"Where do you want to go?" asked the Cat.

"I don't know," said Alice.

"Then," said the Cat, "it really doesn't matter, does it?"

To those seeking a way out of hell, it does matter. It mattered for the children of Israel, for it was only by choosing life and good over death and evil that they could find their way to the Promised Land.

We employ all kinds of means to avoid making such decisions. For example, many individuals would respond to Moses' challenge by saying, "Things just aren't that simple!" In other words, the choices and decisions we are called upon to make are complex and sophisticated; it is not a simple matter of black and white, but a whole conglomerate of shades of gray.

The Bible doesn't change its stance. From this passage in the very first section of the Old Testament to Jesus' confrontation with the rich young ruler, the basic choice is presented as an either/or proposition. In other words, we can't choose both good and evil, heaven and hell, blessing and curse. Of course, there are those who try. They are like the circus act in which the performer places a foot on each of two horses running side by side. But the horses go only in circles.

Life continually urges choices upon us—in politics, foreign policy, municipal problems, personal decisions. When moral issues are involved it is the most natural thing in the world for us to defer a decision. To stand up and be counted is seldom pleasant, for it may cost friendship and understanding, destroy peace of mind, and lay upon us new and unwanted responsibility. Where moral and spiritual issues may be involved, there should be no hesitation. The unending task of a prophet, a teacher, or a preacher is to present our human relationship with God in such a way that no individual can remain blindly neutral. Genuine religion is urgent religion. Moses understood that! He said, "I call heaven and earth to witness against you this day, that I have set before you life and death." No matter how we may attempt to escape this basic choice, sooner or later each of us must face such a challenge—"Sell all that thou hast . . . come and follow me." Jesus stated it differently in other instances, but the impact is the same: "He that is not with me is against me."

Can we really hide behind the lame excuse that the choice is not so simple? I think not! Faith is casting our lot on God's side. That is true whether we are the children of Israel uncertain about moving into the Land of Canaan, or whether we are products of this modern technological age. We may not have any choice over the varied circumstances of our lives, but we do choose how we shall live. If anything, this present age makes the necessity for a basic decision much more crucial.

Legend says that President Abraham Lincoln heard someone express the hope that "the Lord is on our side." Lincoln responded, "It is my constant anxiety and prayer that I and the nation should choose to be on the Lord's side."

I like the way Studdert-Kennedy, the famous English chaplain of the First World War, put it:

How do I know that God is good? I don't.
I gamble like a man. I bet my life

Upon one side in life's great war. I must,
I can't stand out. I must take sides. The man
Who is a neutral in this fight is not
A man.

He continues in this same drift throughout his poem "Faith," ending with these words:

And Good lives on, loves on, and conquers all—
All War must end in Peace. These clouds are lies.
They cannot last. The blue sky is the Truth.
For God is Love. Such is my Faith, and such
My reasons for it, and I find them strong
Enough. And you? You want to argue? Well,
I can't. It is a choice. I choose the Christ.

And so it is for us! Yet we must honestly confess that the choice is not easy. "Go find a son and raise him as a Moslem," Gandhi told the Hindu leader. Jesus said to the young man, "Go sell what you have and give to the poor." Not many do that. But for the few who do, there are the rewards of life, heaven, and blessings.

For those who don't, there is a price to pay. It was a sad day for many football fans when they learned that the 1959 Heisman Trophy winner Billy Cannon had been arrested and had pleaded guilty to the charge of counterfeiting. Billy Cannon, at the time of his arrest, had already been named one of the elite few inducted into college football's Hall of Fame.

I do not know how Dr. Cannon became involved in counterfeiting. I do know he had made a choice, and that choice was destined to deny, rather than affirm his life. Our choices are rarely easy. But when we make the right choice there are rewards.

"But," says the wise man, "there are two sides to every question."

"Yes," answers the fool, "and there are two sides to a sheet of flypaper. But it makes a difference which side the fly chooses."

There are two rather simple principles. First, we do not make our decisions in a vacuum. Our choice is made in the midst of life, a process of growth. So when we face up to the gargantuan proportions of life's basic decision, we need to understand that such a decision must be reaffirmed each day. And we must dare to measure our life each day by our faithfulness to that choice. The nation of Israel faltered and floundered from time to time after entering the land of Canaan. Always, the Bible describes its failure by saying it had forgotten its covenant relation to God.

The second principle is that when we make our choice for life, heaven, and blessing, we are essentially affirming ourselves in the face of life's inequities and our own inadequacies. The choice for Jesus Christ becomes a way of life. I am reminded of what Kathryn Koob wrote after her experience as one of the American hostages held by the Iranian government from November 1979 until January 1981.

Those 444 days became a time of spiritual growth because I had had a lifetime of preparation. . . . From the first time that my hands were folded and I was taught to say "Amen" by my parents, I was guided by them and my grandparents and by the family of Christians that made up my church. The faith that they had shared with me sustained me, by God's grace, when the mobs in the streets by the embassy were screaming, "Death, Death!" I knew I was safe in the love of God. (*Lutheran Standard Magazine* [May 15, 1981]: 9)

Early in her life, Kathryn Koob had made a decision to follow the way of Jesus Christ, and she had reaffirmed that decision daily. She was fortunate to have parents, grandparents, and a church to nurture her and surround her with the spirit of faith. Little wonder that when she heard those fanatical voices screaming, "Death, Death!" a strong vibrant voice within her cried, "Life, Life!" We may never face such a situation, but we are often caught in the depressing inequities of life and the paradox of our own inadequacy. It is then that difficulty recedes into the shadows, and all that matters is that we have indeed made the right choice.

Therefore, "Choose life . . . heaven . . . blessing!" And do it now! Then you will find your way out of the hell in which your very existence has been torture, and life will be affirmed. So be it. So be it now!

CHAPTER 12

The Invitation Has Not Changed!

(The Selflessness of Discipleship)

Mark 8:27-38

Jesus has never been accused of trying to secure followers under false pretenses. On the contrary, you may have heard that he was too brutally frank in his assessment of reality. In other words, Jesus was guilty of what some call overkill. When putting his followers to the test he tended to emphasize the negatives rather than the positives. Public relations people will tell you that possibilities are limited when you take that approach. For all practical purposes, you can forget any mass appeal.

Consider for a moment the real weight of our Scripture from the Gospel of Mark. For more than two years that little band of men had been the daily associates of Jesus. They had experienced the thrill of the crowds. They also had experienced some low moments. However, for the most part, those years had been an exhilarating experience. No one spoke as Jesus did! No one performed the miracles he performed. It was clean and refreshing simply to be in his presence.

In fact, the declarative affirmation seems

almost natural when, in answer to Jesus' question "Who do you say that I am?" the response was, "You are the Christ." Little wonder the disciples wanted to close their ears when Jesus "began to teach them" that he "must suffer." There is nothing cheerful or sensible about a religion that requires suffering. So Simon Peter, spokesman for the disciples, turned on Jesus and began to rebuke him. Jesus would not accept the rebuke. Instead, he used some of the strongest language of his ministry: "Get behind me, Satan! For you are not on the side of God, but of men."

Jesus did not wish to gain disciples under false pretenses. He was not inviting these men to join him in a picnic, but to march with him into the very jaws of hell. His demands were never watered down. When he talked about the cross he did not slur or mumble, but spoke clearly and with conviction.

His invitation today has not changed! It remains the same: "If any man would come after me, let him deny himself and take up his cross and follow me."

In a fallen world, redemption comes hard. It cost God the life of his only Son. Providing salvation for a broken planet inhabited by warped people is an uphill climb. Somewhere, sometime, some must step out of the crowd and thrust themselves on the playing field where the souls of people are at stake. Some must take seriously that ancient Christian claim that one's loyalty to God is the greatest loyalty. And scars and bruises will result from that commitment.

The invitation of Jesus begins with his call to deny ourselves. The word *deny* is not vague. It is a clear, strong term. Only the foolish would think that denying oneself is like giving up chocolate for Lent. To deny ourselves is to put ourselves in a secondary position so that the Kingdom takes priority. It is the change that took place in the prodigal son.

And that change also came over Simon Peter during the confrontation described in Scripture. Peter had struggled with Jesus, trying desperately to control events so that Jesus wouldn't go to Jerusalem. But he needed to learn that his job was not to control anything, especially Jesus. His job was to be obedient. And when he said to Jesus, "You are the Christ," he was being completely obedient. In this sense, Peter was already laying down his life, surrendering himself, dying to self in order to be reborn to Christ.

The invitation of Jesus is an invitation to self-denial. And there can be no self-denial without total commitment. So often our commitments are made with tongue in cheek, with conditional clauses written in small print. This is true also of our commitments to one another.

We need to remember that we are only human beings, in the process of being perfected. God understands this better than we do, and God is patient. God can listen to our confession, knowing full well we will not act accordingly.

Jesus, by pressing his invitation, was helping Peter discover who he really was. As time passed and Peter grew in his faith, he recognized what the apostle Paul came to understand—"It is not I, but Christ." When Peter made his confession that day, he was surrendering himself into the care and keeping of God, admitting his own insufficiency and humbly presenting himself as a servant.

It is important to notice that the invitation of Jesus includes taking up a cross. Many people think the cross we are called upon to bear is always in the form of some calamity or tragedy. Any burden—divorce, death, depression—is described in terms of the cross they have to bear. But I do not believe these are the things Jesus had in mind.

Tragically, I think this has been misunderstood. Christian cross-bearing is deliberately choosing to take up a burden to help a brother or sister in love. It is the grand business of volunteerism. We are compelled by our strong love of God in Jesus Christ. That is taking up the cross!

One man who played the part of Christ in the Passion Play in Oberammergau used a heavy cross in the crucifixion scene. When he was asked why he did not use a lighter one, he replied, "I could not play the part of Christ without feeling the weight of his cross." Christianity has always called us to step forward and support the causes of the Kingdom, not to look for bargain living that avoids cost.

In *Profiles in Courage*, in which John F.

Kennedy related the courageous actions of eight senators, he noted realistically that these men did not act solely for the public good:

It was not because they "loved the public better than themselves." On the contrary it was precisely because they did *love themselves*—because each one's need to maintain his own respect for himself was more important to him than his popularity with others—because his desire to win or maintain a reputation for integrity and courage was stronger than his desire to maintain his office—because his conscience, his personal standard of ethics, his integrity or morality, call it what you will—was stronger than the pressures of public disappoval—because his faith that *his* course was the best one, and would ultimately be vindicated, outweighed his fear of public reprisal.

([Harper & Brothers, 1955], pp. 238-39)

Although Kennedy was not writing from a specific Christian viewpoint, he has nevertheless given us a deep insight into what Jesus had in mind when he talked about taking up the cross. It involves a compulsion toward righteousness, a compulsion which, if denied, leads not to freedom but to slavery—slavery to fear. There is some part of us that does not permit us to experience total freedom until we seek to suffer for others. This is what the New Testament means when it admonishes us to "carry one another's burdens."

Following self-denial and voluntarily taking up a cross, there should be movement. Faith is never static; it is dynamic. The gospel can never be boxed up in a building, for its very nature demands interaction with life on the streets.

When visiting the Holy Land, I was disappointed in the Church of the Nativity, supposedly built over the place where Jesus was born, and the church in Old Jerusalem, supposedly erected on one of the places where it was believed Jesus was buried. Like most old church buildings, they smelled musty. But more than that, they were so ornate that, had there been any truth to be revealed, one could not have recognized it.

Church buildings have their place, but they are way stations which dot the highways of life's challenging road. Jesus began the parable of the talents by illustrating that the kingdom of heaven could be compared to a man going on a journey. The late Bishop Gerald Kennedy has suggested that there is a sense in which that part of the sentence expressed a complete truth. In other words, Jesus invites us to join him on a journey. Deny yourself! Take up your cross! Follow him! And that means follow him all the way.

After a disastrous military charge during the Crimean War, Alfred, Lord Tennyson, was moved to write "The Charge of the Light Brigade." It included these lines:

> Theirs not to make reply,
> Theirs not to reason why,
> Theirs but to do and die.
> Into the valley of Death
> Rode the six hundred.

That poem, and the action that inspired it, have been blasted by many as blind, stupid patriotism. However, there is a truth involved in soldiering that also is basic to life—the simple attribute of obedience. The apostle Paul shared some advice and wisdom with young Timothy: "No soldier on service gets entangled in civilian pursuits, since his aim is to satisfy the one who enlisted him" (II Tim. 2:4).

It matters not whether we offer a cynical sneer in response to that. The truth remains that the invitation of Jesus Christ requires that we be obedient. As Jesus went to the cross, I am sure he looked over his shoulder many times, wondering, "Are those I chose following me?"

And the invitation to discipleship has not changed. Jesus does not water down his requirements. He levels with us. He says, "Who do you say that I am?" And if our answer is, "Thou art the Christ!" he responds, "This is what you must do about it: Deny yourself. Take up the cross. Follow me." Self-sacrifice, or discipline in Jesus Christ, is the one gate that permits us to enter into full self-realization and happiness.